JEWELS

· · · · · · · · · · · · · · · · · · · ·

CHILDREN'S PLAY RHYMES

Selected by Shelley Harwayne
Illustrated by Teresa Farr

For my son, Michael
For my daughter, J. J.
where the poetry began
—S.H.

To my mother, Helen
—T. F.

ACKNOWLEDGMENTS

"Jewels" from *Be My Friend* by Edith Segal. Reprinted by permission of Edith Segal.

"Me and My Ball" © 1994 Marc Matthews from *Caribbean Dozen*. Edited by John Agard and Grace Nichols. Published in the U.S. by Candlewick Press, Cambridge, MA. Reprinted by permission.

"Where Do These Words Come From" ("Hominy, Succotash...") from *If I Had a Paka* by Charlotte Pomerantz. Text copyright © 1982 by Charlotte Pomerantz. By permission of Greenwillow Books, a division of William Morrow and Company, Inc.

"Gee lee, gu lu..." from *Chinese Mother Goose Rhymes* selected and edited by Robert Wyndham, copyright © 1968 by Robert Wyndham. Reprinted by permission of Philomel Books.

"Red, white, and blue" from *Street Rhymes Around the World*, edited by Jane Yolen. Published by Wordsong, Boyds Mill Press, Inc. Reprinted by permission.

"Sawdust Song" from *Arroz Con Leche* by Lulu Delacre. Copyright © 1989 by Lulu Delacre. Reprinted by permission of Scholastic Inc.

"Ev'rybody Loves Saturday Night." Words and Music by Ronnie Gilbert, Lee Hays, Fred Hellerman, Pete Seeger. TRO © Copyright 1951 (Renewed) Folkways Music Publishers, Inc., New York, NY. Used by permission.

Every effort has been made to trace the ownership of all copyrighted materials in this book and to obtain permission for their use.

For information contact:
MONDO Publishing
One Plaza Road
Greenvale, New York 11548

Printed in Hong Kong
95 96 97 98 99 00   9 8 7 6 5 4 3 2 1

Designed by Sylvia Frezzolini Severance
Production by Our House

Library of Congress Cataloging-in-Publication Data

Harwayne, Shelley.
    Jewels : children's play rhymes / compiled by Shelley Harwayne ; illustrated by Teresa Farr.
        p.   cm.
    Summary: A multicultural collection of twenty-one children's play rhymes.
    ISBN 1-57255-028-7 (hardcover : alk. paper). — ISBN 1-57255-029-5 (pbk. : alk. paper)
    1. Rhyming games—Juvenile literature. [1. Jump rope rhymes.
2. Counting-out rhymes. 3. Poetry—Collections.] I. Farr, Teresa, ill.
II. Title.
GR480.H35   1995
398.8—dc20   95-12403
                                                              CIP
                                                              AC

CONTENTS

POEMS

ACTION RHYMES

GAME RHYMES

JUMP ROPE RHYMES

SONG RHYMES

Jewels

Sun on the water,
Sun on the sea,
These are the jewels
You can give to me.

4

Rain on the Green Grass

Rain on the green grass,
And rain on the tree,
Rain on the housetop,
But not on me.

Me and My Ball

Ball jump off of my windowsill
Ball jump off of the floor
Ball jump over granny chair
Ball jump off of the door
Ball jump into granny lap
Ball make granny stop snore

6

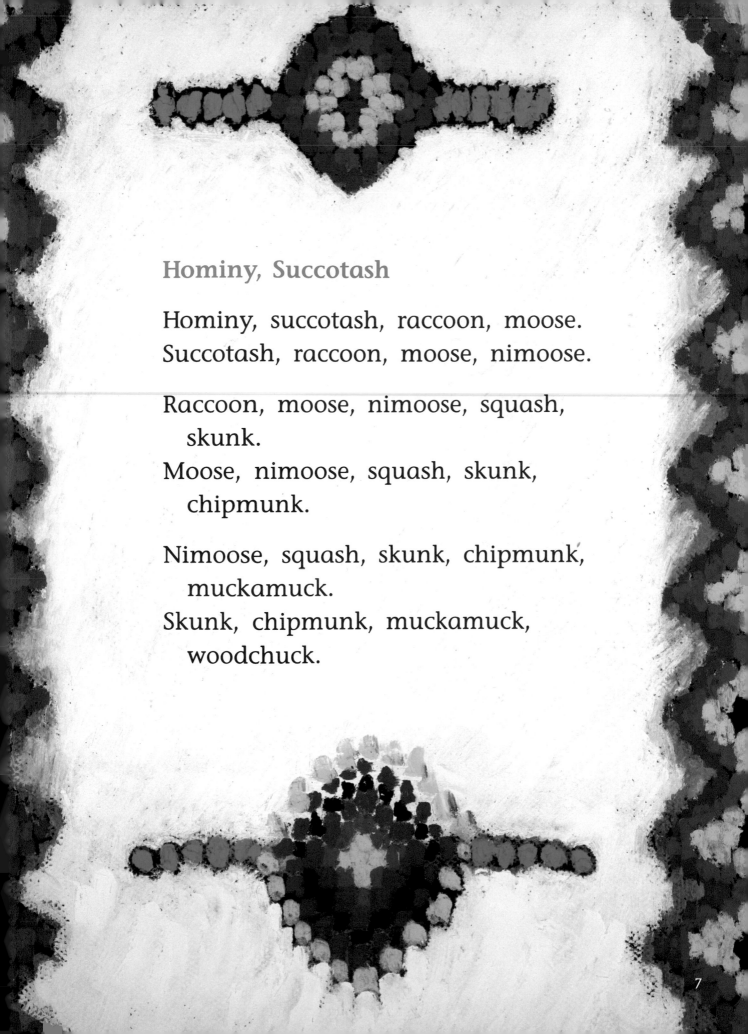

Hominy, Succotash

Hominy, succotash, raccoon, moose.
Succotash, raccoon, moose, nimoose.

Raccoon, moose, nimoose, squash,
  skunk.
Moose, nimoose, squash, skunk,
  chipmunk.

Nimoose, squash, skunk, chipmunk,
  muckamuck.
Skunk, chipmunk, muckamuck,
  woodchuck.

Mary Mack

Oh, Mary Mack, Mack, Mack,
All dressed in black, black, black,
With silver buttons, buttons, buttons,
All down her back, back, back.

She asked her mother, mother, mother,
For fifteen cents, cents, cents,
To see the elephant, elephant, elephant,
Jump over the fence, fence, fence.

He jumped so high, high, high,
That he reached the sky, sky, sky,
And he didn't come back, back, back,
'til the Fourth of July, 'ly, 'ly.

Hot Cross Buns

Hot cross buns! Hot cross buns!
One a penny, two a penny,
Hot cross buns!
If your daughters do not like them
Give them to your sons;
One a penny, two a penny,
Hot cross buns.

10

Patty-cake, Patty-cake

Patty-cake, patty-cake, baker's man,
Bake me a cake as fast as you can.
Roll it and prick it and mark it with B,
Put it in the oven for baby and me.

Pease Porridge Hot

Pease porridge hot,
Pease porridge cold,
Pease porridge in the pot
Nine days old.

Some like it hot,
Some like it cold,
Some like it in the pot
Nine days old.

My Mama's Calling Me

My Mama's calling me.
You can't get out of here.
My Mama's calling me.
You can't get out of here.
What shall I do?
Pat your ones to your knees.
What shall I do?
Pat your twos to your knees,
Pat your threes to your knees,
Pat your all.

Giddy-up, My Little Burro

Giddy-up, my burro,
   we're going to Belén
Fiesta is tomorrow,
   and one next day again.
Hurry, hurry, hurry . . .
Let us go a-pacing,
Hurry, hurry, hurry . . .
Let us go a-racing.
O hurry . . . O hurry . . .

Tin, Tin, Tin, Tin

Tin, tin, tin, tin,
Closed are the doors
Of Don Juan Martín.
Whoever speaks,
Or laughs, or cries,
Must pay a price
Before my eyes.

Eenie, Meenie, Minie, Mo

Eenie, meenie, minie, mo,
Catch a tiger by the toe,
If he hollers, let him go,
Eenie, meenie, minie, mo.

Gee Lee, Gu Lu

Gee lee, gu lu, turn the cake,
Add some oil, the better to bake.

Gee lee, gu lu, now it's done;
Give a piece to everyone.

Sheep in the Meadow

Sheep in the meadow,
Cows in the corn.
Jump in on the month that
  you were born.
January, February, March, April,
May, June, July, August, September,
October, November, December.

Jump Rope, Jump Rope

Jump rope, jump rope,
Will I miss?
Jump rope, jump rope,
Just watch this!

Jelly in the Dish

Jelly in the dish,
Jelly in the dish.
Wiggle, waggle, wiggle, waggle.
Jelly in the dish.

Red, White, and Blue

Red, white, and blue,
Tap me on the shoe;
Red, white, and green,
Tap me on the bean;
Red, white, and black,
Tap me on the back;
All out!

Sawdust Song

Sawdust sings, sawdust songs,
In the woods of Old San Juan.
John eats bread, if you please,
Peter only gets some cheese.
Happy Henry sucks his candy . . .
Almonds spun with sugar candy.

Sally Go Round the Sun

Sally go round the sun,
Sally go round the moon,
Sally go round the chimney tops
On a Saturday afternoon.

Everybody Loves Saturday Night

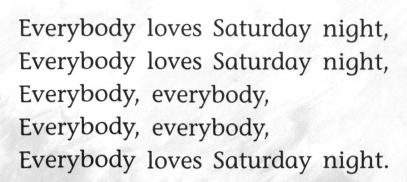

Everybody loves Saturday night,
Everybody loves Saturday night,
Everybody, everybody,
Everybody, everybody,
Everybody loves Saturday night.

Row, Row, Row Your Boat

Row, row, row your boat
Gently down the stream.
Merrily, merrily, merrily, merrily,
Life is but a dream.